SWING TRADING CHART PATTERNS

A STRATEGIC APPROACH TO WINNING TRADES

JAMES WILLY

Copyright © 2024 James Willy

All rights reserved.

TABLE OF CONTENT

INTRODUCTION — 9

Swing Trading Chart Patterns — 9

CHAPTER 1 — 17

Foundations of Forex Swing Trading — 17
- Understanding Swing Trading — 17
- Why Choose the Forex Market — 18
- The Psychology of A Successful Swing Trader — 19
- Essential Tools and Setup — 20
- The Best Time Frames for Swing Trading — 21

CHAPTER 2 — 25

Building Blocks of Chart Analysis — 25
- Understanding Japanese candlesticks — 25
- Price Action Fundamentals — 26
- Support and Resistance — 27
- Market Structure & Trends — 28
- Volume Analysis for Forex — 30

CHAPTER 3 — 33

Basic Chart Patterns — 33

Single Candlestick Patterns	33
Double Candlestick Patterns	34
Triple Candlestick Patterns	35
Early-Stage Trend Reversal Patterns	36
Continuation patterns	37
Candlestick Patterns	40
Hammer and Hanged Man	40
Engulfing Patterns	42
Morning and Evening Stars	45
Doji formations	47
Three White Soldiers, Three Black Crows	47
Shooting Star	50
Chart Patterns	51
Head and Shoulders	51
Double Top / Double Bottom	52
Flag Patterns	54
Triangle Patterns	56
Wedge Patterns	58

CHAPTER 4   61

Advanced Chart Patterns   61

Complex reversal patterns	61
Harmonic Patterns	62
Wave Patterns	63
Multiple Time Frame Pattern Analysis	64
Failed Patterns: What They Tell Us	65

CHAPTER 5 — 69

Entry and Exit Strategies — 69

- Identifying High Probability Setup Points — 69
- Timing your entries — 70
- Strategic Exit Planning — 71
- Partial Position Management — 71
- Scaling into and out of trades — 72

CHAPTER 6 — 77

Risk Management and Position Sizing — 77

- Developing a Risk Management Framework — 77
- Position Sizing Strategies — 78
- Setting Stop Losses — 79
- Managing Drawdowns — 80
- Portfolio Balance and Correlation — 81

CHAPTER 7 — 85

Pattern Integration Strategies — 85

- Combining Multiple Patterns — 85
- Adding Technical Indicators — 86
- Pattern Confirmation Techniques — 87
- Price Action Context — 87
- Creating a Complete Trading System — 88

CHAPTER 8 — 93

Market Context and Timing — 93
    Understanding the Market Phases — 93
    Trading Patterns under Different Market Conditions — 94
    Economic Calendar Impact — 95
    Volatility Considerations — 96
    Seasonal Pattern Analysis. — 96

CHAPTER 9 — 101

Advanced Trading Concepts — 101
    Order Flow Analysis — 101
    Multiple Currency Pair Correlation — 102
    Pattern Failure Analysis — 103
    Advanced Risk-reward Optimisation — 104
    Developing Pattern-Based Trading Systems — 105

CHAPTER 10 — 109

Psychology and Trading Management — 109
    Emotional Control While Pattern Trading — 109
    Developing and Maintaining Confidence — 111
    Creating a Trading Journal — 111
    Performance Analysis and Improvement — 112

CHAPTER 11 — 117

Real-World Applications — 117
    Complete Trade Examples — 117

Pattern Trading Case Studies	118
Common Mistakes and How to Avoid them	119
Adapting to changing market conditions.	120
Developing a Sustainable Trading Career	121

CHAPTER 12 — 125

Beyond the basics — **125**

Developing Your Own Pattern Recognition Skills	125
Developing a Pattern-Based Trading Plan	126
Advanced Money Management Techniques	127
Long-term Success Strategies.	128
Continuous Education and Improvement	128

CONCLUSION — 133

Understanding the Art and Science of Pattern Trading — **133**

Core Pattern Trading Principles	133
The Development of Pattern Trading Skills	134
Risk Management Foundation	134
Integration of Technical Tools	135
Patience & Selectivity	135
Psychological Development	136
Market Adaptation	137
Trading System Integration	137
Continuous Learning	138
Professional Approach	138
Final Thoughts	139

Introduction

Swing Trading Chart Patterns

When I initially saw a flawless double top pattern on the EUR/USD chart, my hands trembled as I entered the trade. After three years of losses and misery, this moment represented a turning point in my forex trading career. The pattern unfolded exactly as expected, and that single trade altered my entire outlook on what was possible in the currency markets.

Pattern trading is more than just recognising shapes on a chart; it is an art form founded on good technical foundations and market psychology.

Through the pages of this book, I'll share my thoughts from almost a decade of trading forex markets using chart patterns, including both the successes and the bitter lessons that formed my journey.

You may be wondering why swing trading specifically. Swing trading, in my perspective, achieves the ideal balance between the frenzied pace of day trading and the long holding periods of position trading. It enables you to record noteworthy moves while living a life that is not confined to your trading displays. I found this after becoming exhausted from day trading in my early years, feverishly attempting to capture every tiny price change.

During the Brexit negotiations, one trade stood out above the rest. I noticed a large inverse head and shoulders pattern on the GBP/USD daily chart. While other traders were caught up in the news, the pattern revealed a clear picture of accumulation.

That trade returned more than 800 pips, but more importantly, it confirmed my trust in the ability of pattern recognition.

The forex market, with its $6.6 trillion daily volume, provides unique opportunities for swing traders. Currency trading's 24-hour nature means that patterns develop and complete more cleanly than in other markets. You'll discover why some patterns work so well in forex while others require adjustment from their traditional stock market roots.

Throughout this book, we will look at patterns ranging from simple candlestick formations to complicated harmonic patterns. But, let me be clear: this isn't just another technical analysis book full of theory. Each pattern discussion is based on real trading experience, and includes extensive examples of both successful and unsuccessful trades.

I've discovered that understanding why a pattern fails is often more important than examining its triumphs.

I recall one pricey lesson with a head and shoulders pattern on USD/JPY. The textbook setting appeared excellent, but I forgot to account for the Bank of Japan's interventionist tendencies. That costly blunder taught me the critical importance of market context, a topic we'll delve into in later chapters.

Risk management is the cornerstone of successful pattern trading. You'll learn how to properly size positions, create reasonable stop losses, and handle trades as they occur. These are not arbitrary rules; rather, they are battle-tested ideas that have repeatedly preserved my trading account. During the 2020 market turmoil, these same concepts saved my capital while others had their accounts wiped out.

One prevalent misperception regarding pattern trading is that it necessitates complex indicators or advanced tools. In actuality, the most dependable patterns emerge through pure price action. I trade largely using clean charts, making judgements based on support and resistance levels, as well as pattern detection. This simplicity fosters consistency, which promotes success.

This book will help you understand how to find high-probability pattern configurations.

• Understanding the psychology behind pattern development and completion.

• Developing risk management approaches for pattern trading.

• Using patterns in conjunction with other technical tools.

• Strategies for trading patterns in various market scenarios.

Becoming a successful pattern trader is a journey that is not linear. My personal journey includes bouts of self-doubt, account withdrawals, and moments of clarity that transformed everything. I will openly share my experiences to help you avoid the dangers that nearly killed my trading career.

Pattern trading in forex necessitates patience, discipline, and a systematic approach. The goal is not to detect as many patterns as possible, but to identify and manage the highest probability configurations. One well-executed trade can outperform dozens of lousy ones, a concept I took years to fully grasp.

In the next chapters, we will progressively improve your pattern recognition skills. We'll start with the fundamentals of price movement and market structure before moving on to more complex topics like harmonic patterns and multi-timeframe analysis.

Each chapter builds on the previous one, resulting in a comprehensive framework for making pattern-based trading decisions.

The markets are continually changing, yet the psychology underlying pattern formation is extremely persistent. This book will teach you how to adapt and prosper in shifting market conditions while keeping the discipline necessary for long-term success.

Let's embark on this journey together, learning the intriguing world of forex pattern trading via the prism of real-life experience and application. The path ahead presents both problems and possibilities; your success will be determined by how you apply these lessons to your own trading journey.

Chapter 1

Foundations of Forex Swing Trading

Understanding Swing Trading

My entire perspective to the forex market was changed the first time I learnt about swing trading. Swing trading hits the sweet spot in between the gruelling demands of day trading and the lengthy waiting periods of position trading. It focusses on price changes lasting several days to a few weeks, ideally coinciding with major market swings while saving you time and energy.

Swing trading is based on a fundamental principle: markets move in waves.

These waves provide opportunities to participate during temporary pullbacks and leave once the dominant trend restarts. My trading changed substantially after I comprehended this principle. Instead of chasing every tiny movement, I learnt to identify and capitalise on major market swings.

Why Choose the Forex Market?

The forex market stands out as an excellent setting for swing trading tactics. Its large daily volume results in smooth price changes that form distinct patterns. Years of market trading have found that currencies frequently respect technical levels more consistently than other instruments.

The 24-hour nature of forex trading minimises the gaps found in stock markets, resulting in cleaner chart patterns and more trustworthy technical analysis.

Major currency pairings such as EUR/USD and GBP/USD have exceptionally well-defined swings, making them ideal candidates for pattern-based trading strategies.

The Psychology of A Successful Swing Trader

Trading psychology is the foundation of successful swing trading. One important lesson I learnt early on: patience trumps action. Many traders feel forced to be in the market continually, but swing trading necessitates the discipline to wait for high-probability situations.

My greatest profitable times have consistently occurred when I keep emotional distance from my trades. This does not imply eliminating emotions; that is impossible. Instead, it's important to acknowledge them while keeping them from impacting your trading selections.

During a particularly difficult moment with USD/JPY, maintaining this emotional equilibrium allowed me to adhere to my plan despite numerous consecutive losses, resulting in a huge winning trade.

Essential Tools and Setup

Your trading setup does not have to be sophisticated. I typically use a clean chart platform, a dependable internet connection, and an organised trading strategy. The main tools include:

A good charting program that provides numerous timeframes and clear visibility of price action. Access to the economic calendar allows you to track major market occurrences. Keep a trading journal to record and analyse your trades. Position size calculator for effective risk management.

The simplicity of this setup allows you to focus on what really matters: price action and pattern recognition. I've seen far too many traders become lost in a jungle of indicators and several screens, losing sight of the fundamental price moves that fuel good trades.

The Best Time Frames for Swing Trading

Through rigorous testing, I found that the forex chart is the best primary time frame for swing trading forex. It gives the best perspective of large market swings while filtering out market noise. Once you've discovered a setup on the daily period, the 4-hour chart is ideal for entry and exit.

My trading improved significantly when I stopped attempting to monitor too many periods at once.

Instead, I take a top-down strategy, using daily charts to identify trends and major patterns, 4-hour charts for timing, and 1-hour charts to fine-tune entry.

One particularly effective strategy is to combine these timeframes during major market movements. During the USD/CHF collapse last year, the daily chart showed a strong downtrend, however the 4-hour chart revealed exact entry points via pullback patterns. This multi-timeframe approach enabled the capture of multiple profitable swings throughout the overall advance.

Understanding these basic principles is the cornerstone for successful forex swing trading. They provide a foundation for all you'll learn about patterns and market analysis. I continue to use these fundamentals on a daily basis, whether I'm trading a simple trend continuation or a complex harmonic pattern.

Mastering these fundamental principles will provide a solid basis for your trading experience. The principles presented here have a direct impact on how you will identify, analyse, and trade the patterns we will study in subsequent chapters. Each successful trades I execute is traced back to these fundamental concepts, highlighting their significance in real-world trading settings.

Chapter 2

Building Blocks of Chart Analysis

Understanding Japanese candlesticks

Japanese candlesticks are the foundation for modern forex chart analysis. During my early trading career, I dismissed candlesticks as extremely unsophisticated. That mistake cost me dearly. Each candlestick tells a story about the conflict between buyers and sellers during a certain time period. A long upper shadow on a bearish candle, for example, shows how buyers first drove prices higher until sellers overpowered them.

The true power of candlesticks is their capacity to reveal market psychology. Consider the doji pattern: a candle with a small body and extended shadows. I once saw this configuration at a major resistance level on the EUR/USD. The hesitation it signalled led to a 200-pip dip, demonstrating how single candlesticks can herald big turning moments.

Price Action Fundamentals:

Price action is the purest type of market analysis. It removes the complexities of indicators to focus on what matters most: how prices change. Through years of trading, I've learnt that price action communicates market participants' intentions more plainly than any indicator.

Raw price movement generates distinct patterns that replicate across currency pairs and timeframes. Certain price formations, such as double tops or false breakouts, behave similarly when trading GBP/USD or USD/JPY.

Price action is an excellent instrument for forecasting future market movements because of its constancy.

Support and Resistance.

Support and resistance levels serve as unseen obstacles in the currency market. These price zones, when buying or selling pressure increases, provide the foundation for profitable trading. My method for identifying these levels focusses on places where prices have regularly reversed.

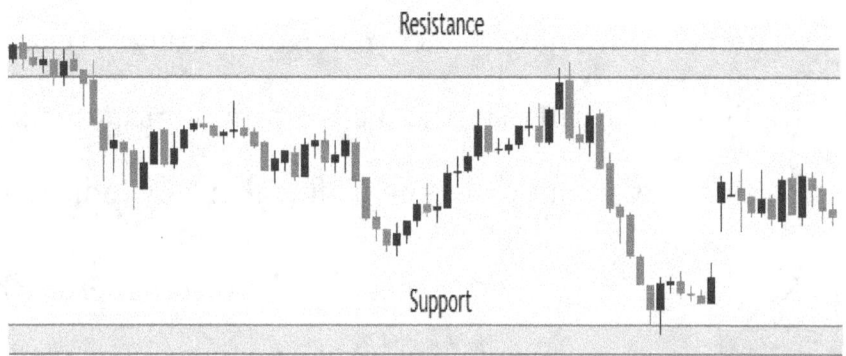

One notable trade had a high resistance barrier on the AUD/USD that rejected the price three times. When the price neared this level again, the following rejection provided an excellent swing trading opportunity. Understanding that support and resistance are not actual prices, but rather zones where market psychology plays a role, is the key.

Market Structure & Trends

Market structure offers context for all trades. It refers to the overall pattern of highs and lows that define trends and trading ranges. Understanding market structure helped me go from trading at random to trading with purpose and confidence.

A trend manifests itself as a series of higher highs and higher lows (uptrend) or lower highs and lower lows (downtrend).

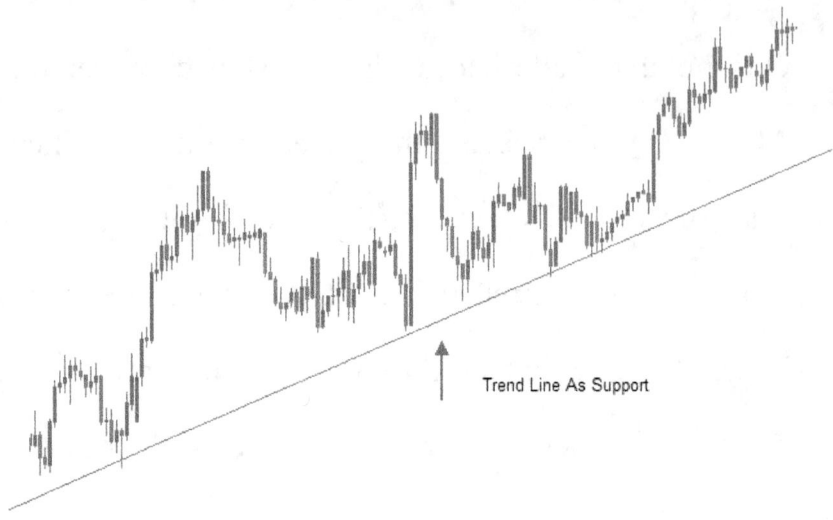
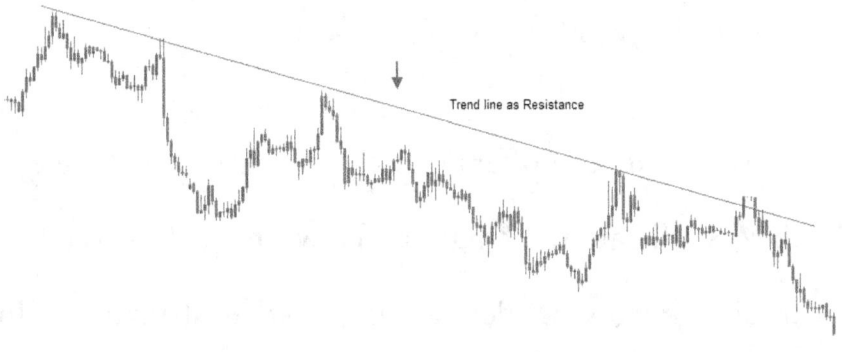

I learnt to recognise these patterns by examining the relationship between swing points. This information was essential during a significant USD/CAD advance, when understanding market structure allowed me to retain positions through modest pullbacks.

Volume Analysis for Forex

Forex volume analysis differs from other markets due to the decentralised structure of currency trading. Rather than actual volume, we examine tick volume or trading activity. This alternative approach nevertheless gives useful information on market involvement and potential reversals.

My experience has shown that combining volume analysis and price action improves trade judgements.

During a recent NZD/USD slide, growing volume during price dips demonstrated significant selling pressure, while declining volume during rebounds indicated weak buying. This confluence of signals generated high-probability trading opportunities.

The relationship between volume and price movement frequently reflects underlying market characteristics. Divergences in price and volume can indicate probable reversals. These indications have been particularly dependable during big market turning times, allowing me to enter trades ahead of significant changes.

These basic elements form the foundation for advanced pattern recognition. A thorough understanding of market behaviour is provided by each component, including candlesticks, price action, support and resistance, market structure, and volume.

When used successfully, they form a strong foundation for spotting high-probability trading opportunities.

Trading success stems from combining various elements rather than relying on a single factor. A strong setup often demonstrates confluence across numerous construction pieces. For example, a bearish engulfing candlestick at resistance, combined with large volume and a breaking market structure, makes a much stronger argument than any single indicator.

Understanding these basics elevates chart analysis above simple pattern recognition to a deeper understanding of market dynamics. Each graphic conveys a story about market participants' actions and objectives. Learning to read these stories through the prism of technical analysis gives you a substantial advantage when identifying winning trading chances.

Chapter 3

Basic Chart Patterns

Single Candlestick Patterns

The mastering of single candlestick patterns indicates the start of more advanced chart analysis. My first large forex profit came from a hammer pattern on USD/CHF, which is a single candle with a lengthy lower shadow and a small body at the bottom of a downward trend. The pattern indicated strong buying pressure, resulting in a 150-pip higher move.

Hammer, shooting star, and marubozu are examples of key single candlestick forms.

Each pattern holds a distinct importance. A shooting star at resistance usually heralds a reversal; I've seen this happen multiple times across different currency pairs. The marubozu, which indicates complete domination of buyers or sellers, typically predicts the beginning of big swings.

Double Candlestick Patterns

Double candlestick patterns increase the intricacy and reliability of our analysis. The encompassing pattern sticks out as very effective. During a recent EUR/USD trade, a bearish engulfing pattern at resistance led to a winning short position. Understanding the psychology behind these patterns is critical, as they demonstrate a definite shift in market control.

The tweezer top and bottom patterns are especially important in FX markets. Their existence at support or resistance levels frequently indicates precise reversal points. These patterns work especially well on 4-hour and daily charts, when market psychology is more consistent.

Triple Candlestick Patterns

Three-candle formations provide deep insights on market psychology. The morning and evening star patterns are among my most consistent arrangements. I recall a morning star formation on GBP/USD, which signalled the end of a steep fall. The steady shift from selling to buying pressure, which occurred across three candles, foreshadowed a significant surge.

The three inside up and three inside down patterns show a progressive shift in market mood. When they form at critical support or resistance levels, their reliability improves.

My trading outcomes increased dramatically after I learnt to combine these patterns with broader market context.

Early-Stage Trend Reversal Patterns

Identifying early trend reversals sets successful traders apart from the crowd. Despite its popularity, the head and shoulders pattern can still be extremely powerful when used correctly. One of my most winning trades resulted from a head and shoulders bottom on the AUD/USD, yielding more than 300 pips as the trend reversed.

The double bottom and double top patterns indicate potential reversals due to failed attempts to break support or resistance. Their power resides in demonstrating the fatigue of the prevailing trend. Trading these patterns taught me patience; waiting for confirmation often results in missing the absolute bottom or top, but it leads to more consistent trades.

Continuation patterns

Continuation patterns create possibilities to join established trends. Flags and pennants are among the most reliable continuation configurations. During a strong USD/CAD rise, a bull flag pattern offered a precise entry point into the move. The measured move notion connected with these patterns makes it easier to set realistic profit targets.

The ascending and descending triangle patterns provide high likelihood continuation signals. Their increasingly shrinking price action reflects the increasing pressure preceding the next move. According to my experience, these patterns are most effective in trending markets with clear direction.

Understanding formation and context is necessary for pattern identification. The reliability of a pattern is heavily influenced by its location within the larger market structure. To properly trade these patterns, several elements must be considered, including market trend, support/resistance levels, volume, and nearby major price levels.

The psychological impact of pattern trading cannot be understated. Each pattern depicts the aggregate actions of market participants. Understanding this psychology aids in anticipating pattern fulfilment and probable failures. I've learnt that patterns often fail when too many traders recognise them; the idea is to look for less obvious setups.

Rather than perfect identification, disciplined execution is the key to pattern trading success. Even the most trustworthy patterns fail on occasion.

Risk management through adequate position sizing and stop placement is more important than pattern accuracy. My most successful time occurred when I concentrated on risk management rather than trying to discover ideal configurations.

These basic patterns lay the groundwork for more complex technical analysis. Mastering them necessitates screen time and experience. Practice and diligent observation will help you build an instinctive sense of pattern reliability and context. The patterns outlined here occur on a regular basis in forex markets, presenting numerous opportunities for those who can identify them.

Pattern trading merges art and science. While the patterns themselves follow particular laws, their interpretation necessitates judgement gained through experience. Each trade setting has unique qualities that determine its chances of success.

Learning to analyse these criteria takes time, but it results in consistently lucrative trading selections.

Candlestick Patterns

Hammer and Hanged Man

The hammer and hanging man patterns have similar structures but communicate distinct stories. During the USD/JPY downturn, I noticed a beautiful hammer with a long lower shadow. The pattern revealed strong buying pressure, with sellers pushing prices lower but buyers regaining control. That single pattern resulted in a 200-pip rally.

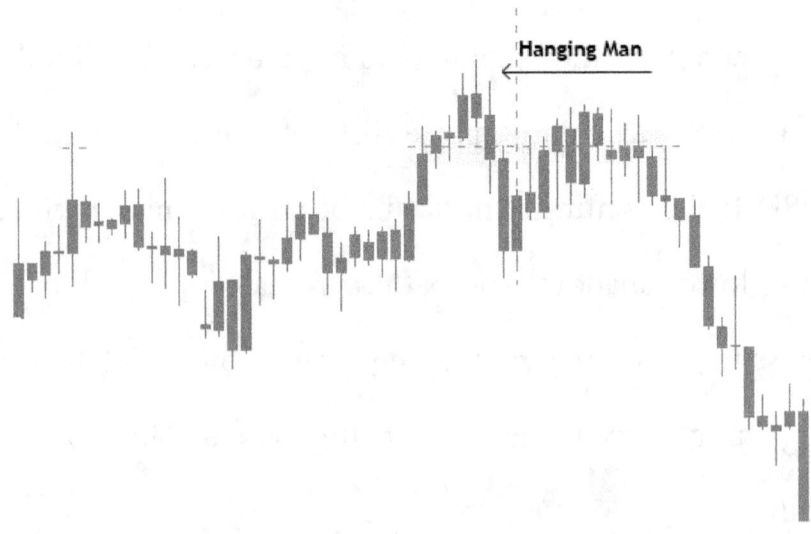

The hanging guy, who appears at market highs, warns of probable reversals. Last month, a hanging man near EUR/USD resistance foreshadowed a steep collapse. The key lies in the long lower shadow, which indicates selling pressure testing the market's strength.

Engulfing Patterns

Bullish and bearish engulfing patterns are among my most consistent setups. A bearish engulfing happens when a red candle totally covers the previous green candle. Trading GBP/USD, I witnessed a bearish engulfment at key resistance. The pattern clearly indicated a move from buying to selling pressure, resulting in a good short position.

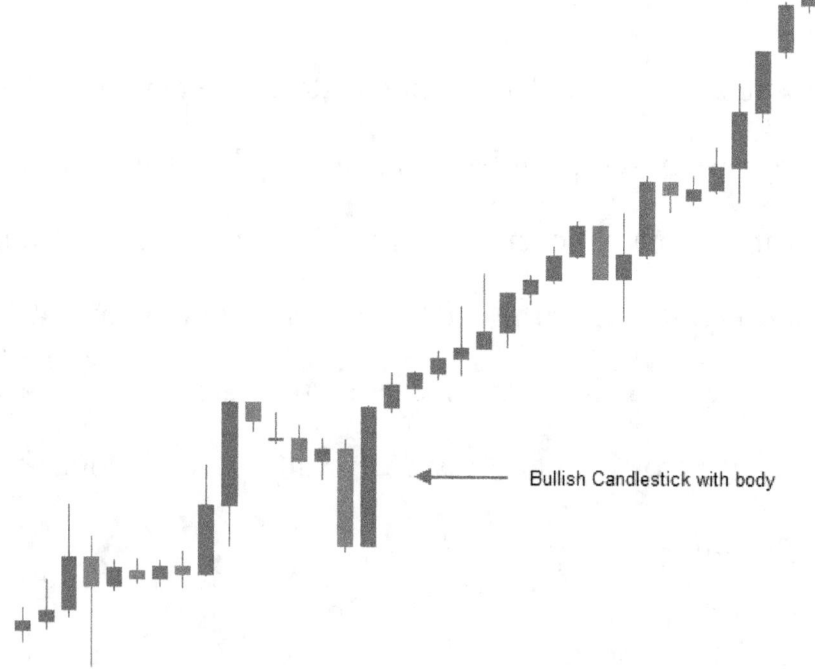

The bullish engulfing shows buyers outnumbering sellers. The pattern's dependability improves greatly when it forms at support levels with stronger timeframe confluence.

Morning and Evening Stars

These three-candle reversal patterns provide intriguing stories about market attitude movements. The morning star begins with a strong bearish candle, then a minor indecisive candle, and ends with a bullish candle. One of my better trades came from a morning star on AUD/USD, which signalled the end of a downturn.

At market peaks, evening stars follow the same pattern. The transition from bullishness to uncertainty to bearishness frequently serves as an early signal of trend reversals.

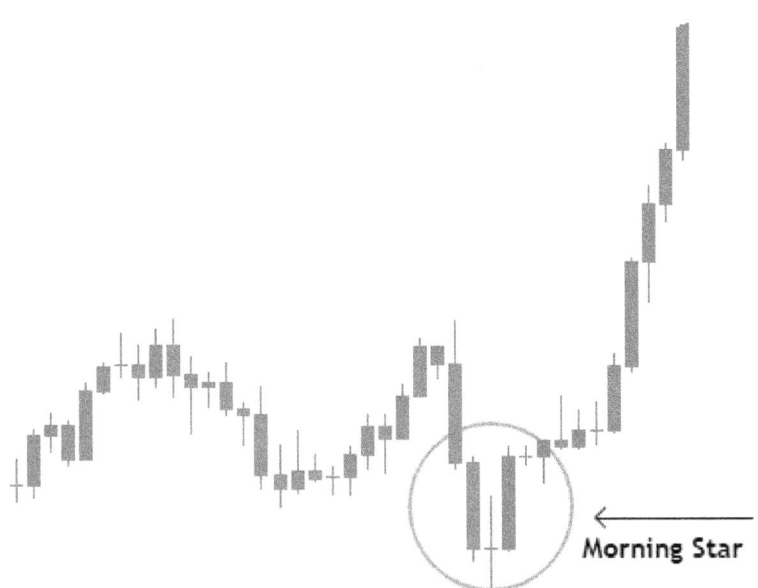

Morning Star

Evening star

Doji formations

Doji candles, with their small bodies and variable shadow lengths, signal market hesitation. The long-legged doji, with prolonged upper and lower shadows, depicts a heated conflict between buyers and sellers. A long-legged doji at resistance foreshadowed a big reversal in the USD/CAD trading pair.

Different forms of doji, such as conventional, dragonfly, and gravestone, each have their own importance. The dragonfly doji, with its long lower shadow, frequently indicates strong buying pressure near market bottoms.

Three White Soldiers, Three Black Crows

These dramatic reversal patterns are made up of three consecutive strong-bodied candles. Three white soldiers demonstrate persistent buying pressure with consecutive bullish candles. Trading NZD/USD, this pattern signalled the commencement of a long-term rise.

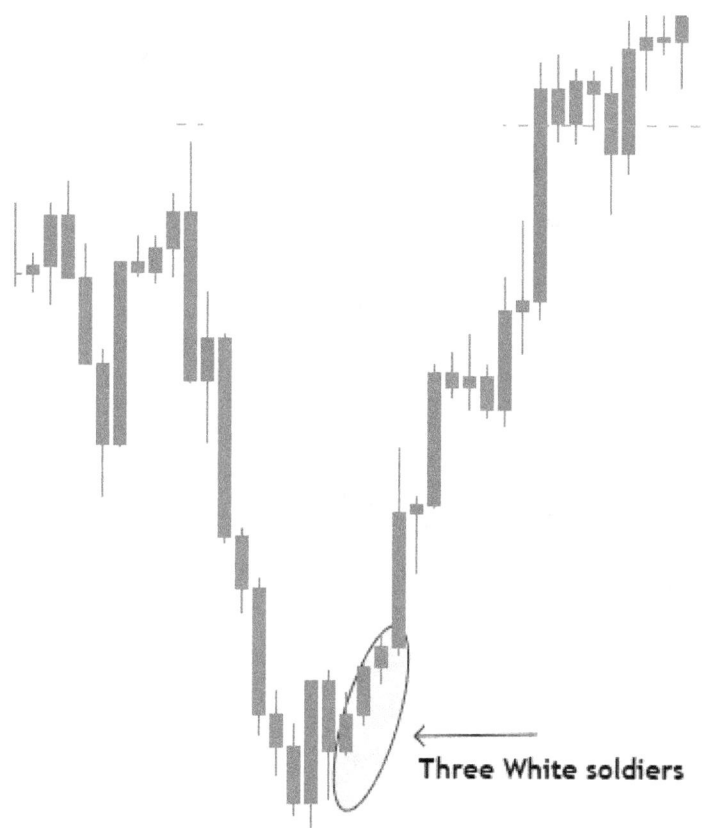
Three White soldiers

In contrast, three black crows indicate strong selling pressure. When the pattern forms after a protracted rise, it is more reliable, often leading to major reversals.

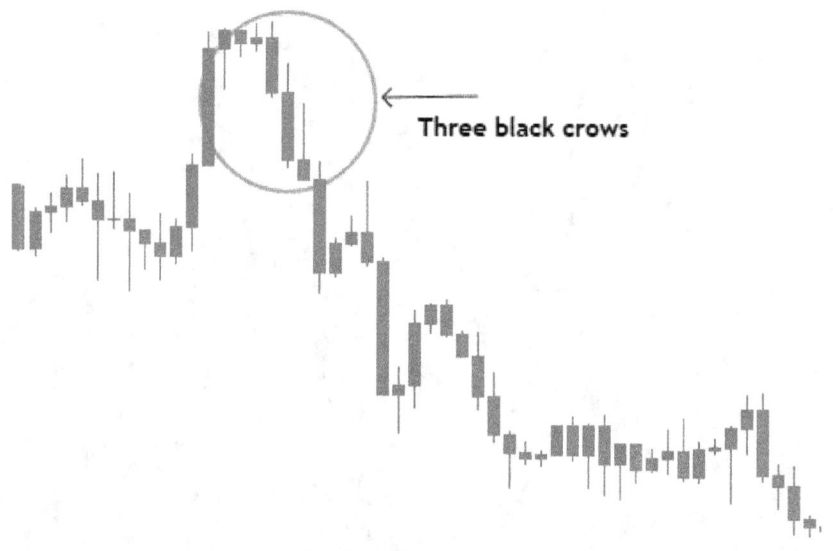

Shooting Star

The shooting star pattern, distinguished by a small body and a long upper shadow, indicates potential trend reversals. During a EUR/USD rise, a shooting star at resistance signalled waning buying pressure. The long upper shadow represented sellers refusing higher pricing.

ENTRY FROM A SHOOTING STAR

Chart Patterns

Head and Shoulders

This classic reversal pattern occurs frequently in FX markets. The pattern comprises of a peak (head) and two lower peaks (shoulders). My most memorable trade was an inverted head and shoulders on USD/CHF, which indicated the end of a long slump.

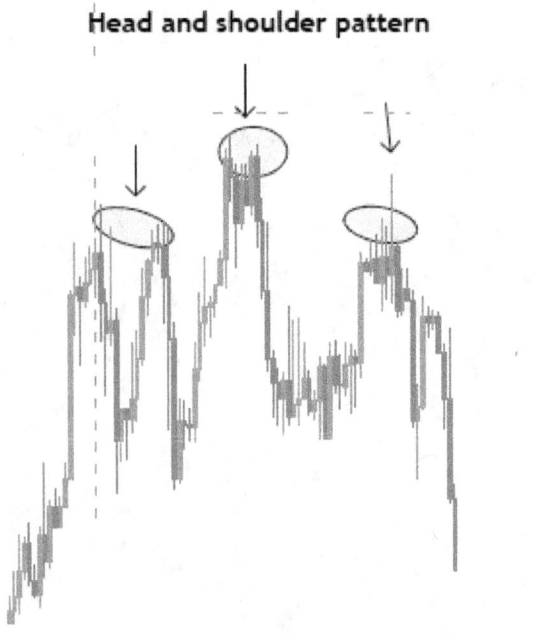

Head and shoulder pattern

The neckline connects the pattern's troughs and acts as an important breakout point. Volume often declines during the pattern's creation and spikes upon breakout.

Double Top / Double Bottom

These patterns indicate trend reversals due to failed attempts to break resistance or support. A double bottom on the GBP/USD resulted in one of my most winning bets. After failing twice to breach support, the second surge surpassed 400 pips.

Double bottom

The key is in the distance between peaks and troughs; broader spacing frequently results in more trustworthy signals.

Flag Patterns

Flags indicate temporary pauses in strong trends. During a strong EUR/USD uptrend, a bearish flag pattern provided an ideal entry point into the move. The pattern's measured motion approach makes it easier to set realistic profit targets.

Bullish Flag

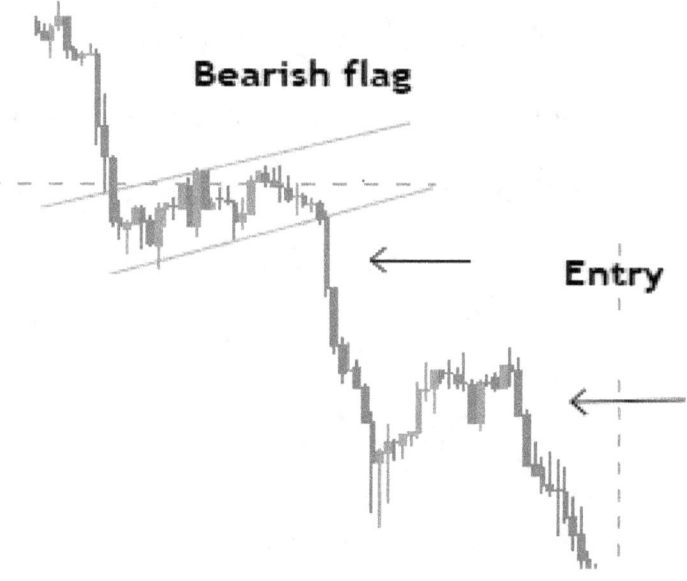

Both bullish and bearish flags indicate orderly price movement against the dominant trend before continuation.

Triangle Patterns

Ascending, declining, and symmetrical triangles indicate gradual shifts in market dynamics. An ascending triangle breakthrough on the USD/JPY pair resulted in a persistent upward advance. The pattern's converging trendlines indicated that buying pressure was building at increasingly higher lows.

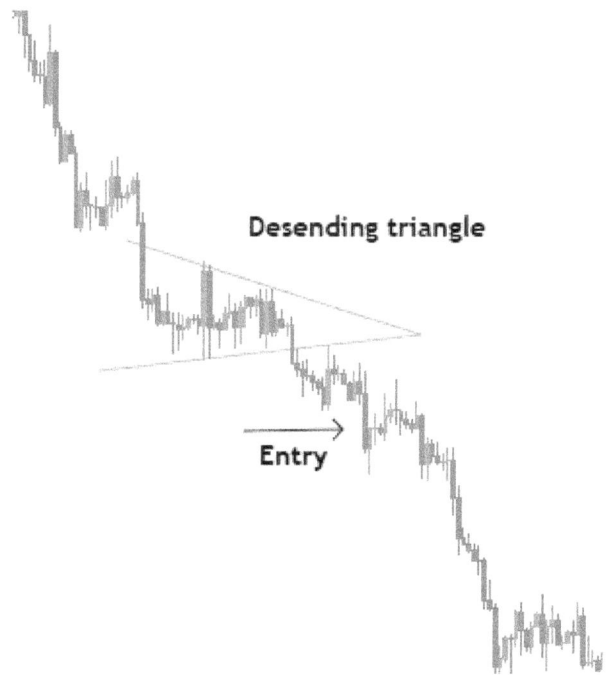

Asending Triangle

Symmetrical triangle

Wedge Patterns

Rising and falling wedges indicate possible reversals via converging trendlines. A rising wedge in a GBP/USD uptrend indicated that momentum was fading ahead of a big fall. The pattern's steadily shrinking price action suggests increasing pressure prior to the break.

Understanding these patterns turns chart analysis from guessing to strategic decision-making. Each pattern reveals a distinct story of market psychology, revealing likely future price movements.

Success is achieved by combining pattern recognition with good risk management and patience in execution.

Chapter 4

Advanced Chart Patterns

Complex reversal patterns

Advanced forex trading necessitates comprehending complicated patterns that frequently indicate major market reversals. The triple top and triple bottom patterns stand out because of their dependability. I found a fantastic triple bottom on EUR/USD, which resulted in a 600-pip rally. Understanding how each failed attempt to breach support diminishes market pressure is critical.

The rounding bottom pattern, sometimes known as a saucer bottom, evolves over time.

Unlike dramatic V-shaped reversals, these patterns reflect subtle changes in market mood. Trading USD/CAD, I saw a rounding bottom form over three weeks before the price began a prolonged rally.

Harmonic Patterns

Fibonacci relationships, which are harmonic patterns, add mathematical precision to technical analysis. The Bat pattern is still one of my favourites because of its precise measurement needs. Each leg must fulfil particular Fibonacci ratios - a 0.886 retracement for point B and a 0.382 extension for point D resulted in a superb setup on GBP/USD last month.

The Gartley pattern, another harmonic creation, corresponds to the Fibonacci levels 0.618 and 0.786. My strategy combines these mathematical levels with supportive price movement.

A Gartley pattern that appears at significant support or resistance is more likely to occur than one in empty chart space.

Wave Patterns

Elliott Wave Theory offers a framework for understanding market cycles. I've learnt from years of trading that perfect five-wave impulse moves are uncommon in FX. However, recognising basic wave shapes aids in predicting potential reversals. A clear three-wave pullback in AUD/USD created a high-probability trade in the direction of the main trend.

The key to wave trading is adaptability. Markets may not always follow textbook patterns, but understanding wave principles allows you to discover high-probability entry points.

During a big USD trend, recognising the completion of wave 4 resulted in profitable entrances into wave 5.

Multiple Time Frame Pattern Analysis

Pattern identification across time frames generates excellent trading setups. A head and shoulders pattern on the daily chart is more significant when backed by smaller patterns on the 4-hour time frame. This multi-layer method enabled me to record a major move in NZD/USD when both time periods coincided.

The secret is to use larger time frames for trend direction and smaller ones for entry timing. When a weekly chart reveals a definite trend, patterns on daily and 4-hour charts provide accurate entry points. This strategy greatly increased my winning percentage on major currency pairings.

Failed Patterns: What They Tell Us

Failed patterns frequently indicate stronger movements in the other direction. A head and shoulders pattern that fails to break its neckline frequently results in strong rallies. My best winning trade was a failed double top on the EUR/USD, which resulted in an upward rise that exceeded all expectations.

Understanding why patterns fail yields useful market information. A pattern failure with significant volume indicates strong opposing pressure. These scenarios frequently result in better trading chances than successful pattern completions. I've learnt from experience that failed patterns might be more profitable than typical arrangements.

The psychology of pattern failure fascinates me. When several traders position themselves for an expected breakout that does not occur, the following squeeze generates strong moves. These events necessitate rapid thinking and immediate action to capitalise on the market's reaction.

Pattern trading at advanced levels necessitates patience and accuracy. Rushing into trades based on partially established patterns causes excessive losses. My trading increased considerably after I began waiting for unambiguous confirmation before entering positions.

Risk management becomes even more important with advanced patterns. Their intricacy creates additional possible failure sites. I always size positions based on the distance to logical stop levels rather than attempting to force trades inside established risk limitations.

Successful pattern trading includes technical analysis and an understanding of market psychology. Each pattern depicts the aggregate actions of market participants. You can build an instinctive sense for market behaviour by analysing both successful and failed patterns.

Advanced patterns necessitate continuous learning and adaptability. Markets change, and patterns that worked well in the past may become less effective. Maintaining flexibility and modifying your approach based on market conditions leads to constant profits.

The journey to learn advanced patterns is never fully over. Even after years of trading, I'm discovering new nuances in pattern development and completion. This ongoing learning process keeps pattern trading interesting and beneficial for those who put in the effort.

Chapter 5

Entry and Exit Strategies

Identifying High Probability Setup Points

The secret of successful forex trading is recognising excellent entry points. Through years of pattern trading, I've noticed that the best setups occur when numerous things align. A recent EUR/USD trade demonstrated this perfectly: a bullish engulfing pattern emerged at support, accompanied by a completed harmonic pattern and oversold conditions.

Your entry strategy must adapt to changing market conditions.

During trending markets, buying pullbacks to support and selling rallies to resistance produce consistent results. One very successful strategy is to enter during the initial downturn following a strong trend break. This strategy detected a significant move in GBP/USD last quarter.

Timing your entries

Precise entry timing distinguishes good trades from frustrating ones. The 'spring' setup is one of my favourite entry tactics, in which price temporarily breaks support before reversing rapidly higher. This fake breakout ensnared many sellers on USD/JPY, resulting in a strong upward move.

Volume confirmation is critical for entry timing. Strong volume on pattern breakouts improves reliability greatly. My success rate increased considerably when I began waiting for volume confirmation before entering trades.

Strategic Exit Planning

Exit tactics frequently have a greater impact on profitability than entries. Trailing stops based on swing points safeguard profits while enabling trends to emerge. During a strong AUD/USD rally, placing stops below each successive swing low protected most profits while avoiding premature exits.

Taking partial profits at logical resistance levels promotes a favourable trade expectation. This method saved numerous trades that later reversed. On a recent NZD/USD position, selling half at key resistance resulted in profits before price consolidation.

Partial Position Management

Managing jobs in parts provides flexibility. Taking partial profits at predefined levels and saving a portion for longer moves maximises return possibilities. This strategy proved helpful in volatile market situations, allowing for profit capture while remaining exposed to wider trends.

The three-part exit strategy has worked very well for me: close one-third at the first target, another third at a major resistance level, and let the final piece run with a trailing stop. This balanced approach routinely generates strong risk-adjusted returns.

Scaling into and out of trades

Strategic position building improves trade management alternatives. Adding to winning trades as confirmation develops boosts profit potential while keeping risk levels manageable. A USD/CAD trend trade began tiny but developed significantly as price action supported the move.

Scaling out necessitates equivalent precision. Reducing position size and increasing strength saves profits while keeping skin in the game. Experience taught me to build out more aggressively in range markets than in strong trends.

Market factors define the most effective scaling options. In volatile markets, faster scaling lowers susceptibility to reversals. Strong trends allow for more slow position reduction, which maximises profit potential from long-term moves.

The psychology of scaling requires discipline. Fighting the impulse to add too quickly or hold positions for too long is a problem for every trader. My most effective times occurred when I followed predetermined scaling principles, regardless of emotional urges.

Scaling choices are supported by technical tools. Moving averages, Fibonacci levels, and chart patterns serve as objective reference points for position adjustments. These tools helped move much of the guesswork out of scaling decisions.

Risk management is crucial throughout the scaling process. Each position addition must be consistent with the overall account risk parameters. One unpleasant lesson taught me to never exceed the maximum risk level, no matter how good the arrangement looked.

Successful entry and exit execution necessitates planning and patience. Predefined strategy for various market conditions reduce emotional decision-making when pressured. Stop making impulsive entries and exits, and your trading performance will substantially improve.

The link between entries and exits results in a full trading strategy. Strong entries mean little without solid exit strategy. Similarly, perfect exits cannot undo bad entry selections. The interaction of entry and exit tactics determines long-term profitability.

Advanced traders understand that good entry and exit points rarely correspond to exact peaks and bottoms. Attempting to catch every pip sometimes results in missed opportunities. Instead, focus on capturing the meat of the move with intelligent entry timing and controlled exit execution.

Chapter 6

Risk Management and Position Sizing

Developing a Risk Management Framework

Risk management is the cornerstone of FX trading success. My early trading experience taught me this lesson the hard way: a succession of overleveraged positions wiped me months' worth of earnings in a matter of days. A strong risk management strategy safeguards your wealth during unavoidable losing streaks while allowing profitable trades to thrive.

Understanding your maximum tolerated drawdown is essential for efficient risk management.

Through years of trading, I've discovered that limiting risk to 1-2% per trade keeps emotions under control while protecting funds for future possibilities. This strategy protected my account under tumultuous market conditions, when multiple trades went against me at the same time.

Position Sizing Strategies

Position sizing has a direct impact on trading psychology and performance. The appropriate position size enables you to remain sensible when trades go against you. Trading EUR/USD last month, my tight position sizing criteria kept me from panicking and exiting a temporarily losing trade that turned out to be extremely beneficial.

Your position size must match the current market volatility. During high-impact news events, limiting position size ensures consistent risk exposure.

One particularly significant lesson I learnt while trading USD/JPY during a Bank of Japan intervention was that smaller positions enabled me to survive high volatility.

Setting Stop Losses

Strategic stop placement balances protection against premature exits. Technical stops based on swing points or chart patterns indicate sensible exit points. A recent GBP/USD trade exemplified this perfectly: setting the stop below a big swing low safeguarded the position while allowing it to grow.

Volatility-based stops respond to shifting market conditions. Using Average True Range (ATR) to set stop distances protects against regular market volatility. This dynamic strategy worked exceptionally well while trading cross-rates with variable volatility levels.

Managing Drawdowns

Drawdown management distinguishes successful traders from others who blow up their accounts. The trick is to recognise when to cut position size or temporarily halt trading. During my greatest downturn phase, taking a step back to examine my technique saved additional losses and resulted in considerable changes to my trading approach.

Recovery from drawdowns necessitates patience and discipline. Attempting to recover losses rapidly through larger positions frequently results in tragedy. Instead, concentrate on regularly executing your strategy with appropriate position sizing; the recovery will occur gradually.

Portfolio Balance and Correlation

Understanding currency pair correlations reduces overexposure to similar market movements. Trading linked pairs such as EUR/USD and GBP/USD together might increase risk beyond acceptable limits. My risk management system now includes correlation checks before accepting new employment.

Portfolio balance goes beyond correlation management. Mixing trending and ranging strategies across currency pairs lowers overall portfolio volatility. This diversification enabled consistent earnings even when single strategies underperformed.

Professional management is required for your trading account, just as it is for any real business.

Monitor crucial indicators such as win rate, average win/loss ratio, and maximum drawdown. These statistics identify areas for improvement while also verifying effective techniques.

Risk management influences all aspects of trading performance. Poor risk management impairs even the most effective trading strategies. I've seen outstanding technical analysts fail because they were unable to manage position sizing and risk exposure.

The psychological benefits of effective risk management cannot be understated. Trading with suitable position sizes decreases emotional stress and allows for clearer decision-making. Many struggling traders improved their outcomes simply by enforcing stringent risk management guidelines.

Successful traders see risk management as a means of managing opportunities. Each trade reflects a calculated risk with predefined criteria. This perspective changes the emphasis away from avoiding losses and towards properly managing trade opportunities.

The dynamic nature of FX markets necessitates adaptive risk management. Adjusting position sizes and risk criteria in response to market conditions ensures constant exposure levels. Your risk management framework should adapt to market changes while keeping basic principles.

Experience and discipline help to build expertise of risk management. Begin with conservative position sizes and progressively expand exposure as results demonstrate consistency. This measured strategy boosts confidence while preserving capital during the learning process.

Chapter 7

Pattern Integration Strategies

Combining Multiple Patterns

Pattern integration takes trading beyond simple pattern detection to strategic analysis. My best profitable trades frequently occur when many patterns align. Last month, a head and shoulders pattern on EUR/USD became significant when a bearish engulfing candle emerged at the right shoulder, resulting in a strong sell signal.

The synergy of many pattern patterns improves trading decisions. Harmonic patterns mixed with regular chart patterns result in exact entry locations.

One noteworthy trade comprised a Gartley pattern closing around the neckline of an inverse head and shoulders on GBP/USD, resulting in a 400-pip profit.

Adding Technical Indicators.

Technical indicators are used as pattern confirmation aids rather than major decision drivers. The Relative Strength Index (RSI) uses divergence analysis to confirm pattern signals. During a USD/JPY rally, negative RSI divergence at a double top pattern indicated a significant reversal.

Moving averages help pattern trading by providing dynamic support and resistance levels. The 50-day moving average is typically used as a reference point for pattern completion. A recent AUD/USD trade was successful when the price bounced off this average during a bull flag formation.

Pattern Confirmation Techniques

Volume analysis confirms significant patterns. Strong volume on breakouts improves pattern dependability greatly. Trading NZD/USD, I observed how dropping volume during pattern creation was followed by a volume increase on breakout, resulting in prolonged swings.

Time analysis provides another level of confirmation. Long-term patterns are frequently more trustworthy than fast forms. My success rate increased significantly when I prioritised patterns that required several days or weeks to finish.

Price Action Context

The price action context influences the pattern's validity. The same pattern produces diverse outcomes based on its location within bigger market systems.

A double bottom pattern at significant support has greater significance than one in the middle of a trading range.

Support and resistance levels influence pattern development. Strong patterns frequently form around important price levels. A complex head and shoulders pattern completed around annual resistance, resulting in a good USD/CAD trade.

Creating a Complete Trading System

Pattern integration develops a comprehensive trading strategy. Your system should integrate pattern identification, risk management, and market analysis. After years of trading, I've modified my system to need many confirmations before initiating trades.

The integration procedure necessitates patience and testing. Not every pattern combination is applicable in all market conditions. During high volatility situations, simpler pattern configurations frequently outperform complicated combinations.

Momentum analysis greatly enhances pattern trading. Strong momentum towards pattern completion frequently indicates strong breakouts. My trading outcomes increased after I incorporated momentum measurements into pattern analysis.

The psychological aspect of pattern integration requires consideration. Complex analysis can lead to analysis paralysis. Your system must strike a balance between thoroughness and decisiveness; too many necessary confirmations can result in missed chances.

Time frame alignment enhances pattern signals. When patterns align across numerous time periods, the chance increases dramatically. Trading EUR/USD using daily chart patterns with 4-hour confirmations yielded consistent results.

Position management responds to pattern complexity. More sophisticated setups may have bigger stops to handle normal market volatility. Experience taught me how to modify position sizing based on pattern type and market conditions.

Pattern failures offer useful insights on system improvement. Failed patterns frequently lead to strong moves in the other direction. Some of my best trades resulted from rapidly recognising and responding to pattern failures.

Understanding market dynamics, rather than memorising settings, is the key to successful pattern integration. Each market session has unique elements that influence pattern development. Your trading system must adapt to changing situations while adhering to its key principles.

The evolution of your trading system is never fully complete. Markets evolve, necessitating continuous improvement of pattern integration tactics. Maintaining flexibility and being open to new approaches while sticking to tried-and-true procedures leads to long-term profitability.

Chapter 8

Market Context and Timing

Understanding the Market Phases

Markets go through diverse phases, which have a direct impact on pattern effectiveness. I've learnt over a decade of trading that understanding the current market phase significantly enhances trades selection. During a recent EUR/USD accumulation phase, typical breakout patterns failed repeatedly until the market began to markup.

The four key market phases - accumulation, markup, distribution, and markdown - each necessitate distinct trading strategies. Range-bound patterns produce greater results than trend-following methods during accumulation phases. My trading performance improved dramatically after I began tailoring pattern choices to market phases.

Trading Patterns under Different Market Conditions.

Pattern dependability varies according to market conditions. During trending markets, continuation patterns such as flags and pennants have higher success rates. Trading bull flags on GBP/USD amid a strong advance proved to be a particularly rewarding period; each pattern presented clear entry points for entering the trend.

Diverse markets necessitate diverse pattern approaches. Double tops and bottoms perform particularly effectively in sideways markets. A number of successful USD/JPY trades resulted from trading range-bound patterns, while other traders struggled with failed breakouts.

Economic Calendar Impact

Major economic releases alter market behaviour. Pattern trading during high-impact news takes careful analysis. When trading patterns approach important announcements, my strategy is to reduce position size and broaden stops.

The aftermath of news events frequently produces predictable patterns. Post-NFP price movement on USD pairings frequently leads to tradeable patterns.

One notable trade involved a beautiful head and shoulders pattern that appeared following a major Fed pronouncement.

Volatility Considerations

Market volatility has a direct impact on pattern creation and completion. High volatility periods can result in faster but less consistent patterns. During the height of market stress last year, focussing on longer-term patterns helped maintain consistency as shorter-term patterns grew chaotic.

Low volatility phases necessitate patience and precision. Patterns take longer to build, but they generally result in cleaner moves. Trading NZD/USD during a period of low volatility, I noticed that price action produced more consistent chart patterns despite slower development.

Seasonal Pattern Analysis.

Pattern behaviour is affected by seasonal inclinations. Certain currency combinations exhibit repeated patterns in specific months. Years of tracking revealed that USD/CAD frequently creates consistent patterns throughout specific seasonal transitions.

Market liquidity fluctuates seasonally, influencing pattern dependability. Year-end trading requires special attention because reduced liquidity can lead to pattern failures. Adjusting position sizing during these times helped to preserve capital while allowing for trading opportunities.

The time of day has a significant impact on pattern development. Asian session patterns differ from those that emerge during the London or New York hours. My most consistent results come from matching pattern trades to appropriate trading sessions.

The combination of many market factors generates unique trading chances. Combining seasonal analysis and pattern recognition improves trade selection. Recognising how seasonal factors influenced pattern completion led to several good trades.

Pattern dependability varies over market cycles. Understanding these correlations aids in optimising trade time. Your success in pattern trading is largely dependent on recognising when specific patterns are most likely to occur.

The market context provides a framework for pattern interpretation. The same pattern produces varied results depending on market conditions. Through experience, I've learnt to evaluate patterns in the context of a larger market rather than in isolation.

Trading success necessitates adjusting to shifting market conditions. Rigid adherence to single pattern types reduces opportunities. My trading increased considerably when I started modifying pattern selection based on current market conditions.

The complexity of market timing necessitates regular attention. Multiple factors determine pattern success rates. Understanding these links takes time, but it produces more consistent trading results.

Pattern trading brilliance is achieved by combining technical talents with market understanding. Each market phase brings distinct problems and opportunities. The capacity to modify pattern trading tactics to current conditions is critical to long-term success.

Chapter 9

Advanced Trading Concepts.

Order Flow Analysis

Order flow gives us a better understanding of pattern development and completion. Years of trading have taught me that understanding order flow improves pattern trading greatly. During a recent EUR/USD scenario, heavy limit orders seen at support increased the likelihood of a double bottom pattern.

The interaction of several order types influences price activity. Stop orders gathering above resistance can cause false breakouts.

One exceptionally profitable trade occurred when the price soared through resistance, triggered stops, and then reversed rapidly, creating the ideal trap for breakout traders.

Multiple Currency Pair Correlation

Currency correlations reveal hidden trading opportunities. Trading correlated pairs requires an understanding of their market linkages. A head and shoulders pattern on USD/CHF became significant when EUR/USD exhibited equivalent weakness via inverse correlation.

Cross-pair analysis identifies leading indicators for pattern trading. Currency movements frequently predict probable patterns in other currency pairs. My trading outcomes significantly improved after including correlation analysis into pattern recognition.

Pattern Failure Analysis

Failed patterns frequently indicate stronger movements in the other direction. I've learnt from experience that pattern failures can provide useful market information. A recent failed triangle pattern on GBP/USD resulted in a strong trend move; the failure itself produced a trading opportunity.

Understanding why patterns fail can improve trading decisions. Common failure causes include a lack of volume confirmation, a poor market setting, or nearby substantial support/resistance. These insights can help you avoid low-probability setups and find potential reversal opportunities.

Advanced Risk-reward Optimisation

Risk-reward ratios respond to pattern characteristics. Different patterns necessitate distinct methods to position sizing and profitability aims. Trading USD/JPY taught me that harmonic patterns typically enable for tighter stops than standard chart patterns, resulting in better risk-reward ratios.

Position sizing grows more complicated with experience. Instead of using predetermined percentages, size positions according to pattern reliability and market conditions. This dynamic method maximises opportunities while ensuring stable risk levels.

Developing Pattern-Based Trading Systems

Systematic pattern trading requires explicit rules. Your system should establish clear criteria for pattern recognition, confirmation, and execution. Through years of development, my trading system grew from simple pattern detection to thorough trading analysis.

Integrating several time periods improves system reliability. Patterns that align across multiple time frames indicate greater probability setups. One effective strategy is to use weekly charts to determine trend direction, daily charts to identify patterns, and 4-hour charts to time entries.

Pattern trading systems offer chances for automation. While comprehensive automation remains difficult, several aspects benefit from methodical techniques.

Price alerts for prospective pattern setups serve to ensure consistency in pattern recognition.

The psychology of system trading requires discipline and patience. Strict commitment to system norms frequently clashes with emotional inclinations. My most prosperous eras have consistently resulted from pursuing systematic procedures rather than gut feelings.

Advanced pattern trading is a combination of technical analysis and market psychology understanding. Each pattern indicates collective trading behaviour. Reading these patterns efficiently requires both analytical and psychological skills.

Pattern complexity grows with experience level. Simple patterns enable the recognition of more complex forms. Trading success depends on matching pattern complexity to your skill level while keeping risk management discipline.

The evolution of trading platforms never stops. Markets fluctuate, necessitating ongoing system refinement. Your strategy must adapt to changing situations while adhering to fundamental principles that ensure consistent profitability.

Advanced pattern trading requires ongoing learning and modification to be successful. Markets change, creating new difficulties and possibilities. The most effective traders maintain flexibility while expanding on established themes.

The interaction of different trading factors results in synergy. Technical analysis, risk management, and psychological elements work together to produce excellent trading results. Understanding these correlations helps improve overall trading performance.

Chapter 10

Psychology and Trading Management

Emotional Control While Pattern Trading

Trading psychology distinguishes successful traders from those who struggle. My early years taught me that emotional control is more important than technical analysis. Maintaining patience during a series of losing trades during a heated EUR/USD trading session ultimately resulted in capturing a significant reversal move.

Fear and greed provide the greatest hurdles in pattern trading. These emotions frequently result in premature exits or delayed entrances. The key is developing a mechanical attitude to trade execution: when a valid pattern emerges with sufficient confirmation, enter the trade regardless of recent performance.

handling Winners and Losers Managing successful trades demands different psychological skills than handling losses. The desire to take immediate profits frequently precludes capturing larger moves. Trading GBP/USD taught me to let profitable trades run while focussing on technical exit indications rather than profit targets.

Losing trades put emotional discipline to the ultimate test. The urge to move stops or average down can devastate trading accounts. Through hard experience, I realised that tolerating tiny losses saves wealth for future opportunities.

Developing and Maintaining Confidence

Confidence stems from consistent execution rather than trading success. Your ability to adhere to trading guidelines determines long-term success. Following a streak of losses on the USD/JPY, maintaining faith in my tried-and-true technique resulted in an impressive rebound.

Overconfidence is as dangerous as self-doubt. Trading success can lead to complacency and ineffective risk management. One particularly bitter lesson came from expanding position sizes after a winning streak; the subsequent losses erased months of profits.

Creating a Trading Journal

Detailed trade journaling exposes patterns in your trading results.

Not only should you record your entrances and exits, but also your emotional state and market conditions. My trading changed when I began researching the relationship between psychological elements and trade outcomes.

The notebook becomes an effective tool for improvement. Reviewing previous trades objectively reveals strengths and faults. Regular journal analysis helped me recognise how particular market conditions influenced my decision-making process.

Performance Analysis and Improvement

Statistical analysis provides information on trading effectiveness. Monitor crucial indicators such as win rate, average win/loss ratio, and maximum drawdown. These data highlight areas for improvement while also verifying effective techniques.

Pattern trading necessitates ongoing self-assessment. Regular reviews of trading performance reveal opportunities for improvement. Through methodical analysis, I discovered unique patterns that regularly provided higher results in certain market scenarios.

Your psychological state has a direct impact on pattern recognition ability. Stress and weariness can result in missed chances or incorrect pattern detection. Learning to recognise these conditions can help you decide when to stop trading.

Trade management gets more difficult during volatile times. When positions are stacked against you, emotional control is put to the ultimate test. Creating guidelines for various market circumstances helps to retain discipline under pressure.

Risk management and psychology have a long history of relationship. Position sizing decisions are often influenced by emotional states rather than logical analysis. Implementing stringent risk parameters alleviates much of the emotional load of trading decisions.

Balancing technical and psychological aspects is necessary for successful pattern trading. Even great pattern identification is meaningless without adequate emotional control. Your ability to retain discipline during winning and losing streaks impacts long-term profitability.

The path to psychological improvement is never-ending. Markets always bring new obstacles for emotional control. Developing and maintaining healthy trading psychology involves consistent work and self-awareness.

Pattern trading mastery combines technical and psychological power. Every trading day provides opportunities to practise both aspects.

Consistent success comes from developing these talents concurrently while maintaining a focus on long-term improvement.

Chapter 11

Real-World Applications

Complete Trade Examples

Theory becomes reality through actual trade execution. A recent EUR/USD setup precisely demonstrated this: a head and shoulders pattern emerged on the daily chart, but the 4-hour timeframe revealed a bearish engulfing candle at resistance. Entry occurred following neckline breakage, with stops placed above the right shoulder. The trade yielded 250 pips as the price approached the measured objective.

USD/JPY gave another illuminating illustration in the form of a failed pattern trade. When the Bank of Japan intervened, what appeared to be a flawless double bottom collapsed. The planned stop loss avoided significant losses, demonstrating the importance of strict risk management even in seemingly favourable situations.

Pattern Trading Case Studies

The importance of patience and precision was demonstrated by a GBP/USD harmonic pattern trade. The Gartley pattern closed at key resistance, coinciding with bearish divergence on the RSI. The initial position sizing at 1% risk allowed for additional profits as price movement confirmed the idea. Multiple scale-outs generated profits while remaining exposed to the broader move.

Cross-pair correlation improved a complex EUR/AUD setup. The daily chart showed a falling triangle, and USD pairs indicated broader dollar profits. Position entry divided between the initial pattern breakout and the subsequent pullback enhanced overall trade performance. Market context and correlation research were critical for trade management decisions.

Common Mistakes and How to Avoid them

Pattern trading necessitates great discipline, but emotional urges sometimes overwhelm logical conclusions. One costly lesson was to ignore volume confirmation on a NZD/USD breakthrough trade. The resulting whipsaw showed why repeated confirmations are more important than jumping into seemingly obvious setups.

Position sizing errors are among the most hazardous blunders. Trading USD/CAD, I once boosted my position size after several successful trades, breaking my risk management principles. The subsequent loss reversed weeks of profits, emphasising the importance of maintaining consistent position sizing regardless of recent results.

Adapting to changing market conditions.

Markets always evolve, necessitating adaptable trading strategies. During instances of strong volatility, widening stops and reducing position size provide consistent risk exposure. A USD/CHF trade during market volatility was successful due to proper position sizing and pattern validation.

Pattern dependability varies with market conditions. Ranging markets like reversal patterns, whilst trending markets perform better with continuation patterns. AUD/USD trading experience demonstrated how modifying pattern selection to the current market phase greatly enhances success rates.

Developing a Sustainable Trading Career

Long-term success necessitates approaching trading as a business. Professional traders keep thorough records, manage risks properly, and constantly improve their skills. Developing these professional practices helped my own journey from struggling rookie to consistent profitability.

Capital preservation takes precedence above profit maximisation. Small losses and regulated risk enable survival during challenging times.

Trading over many market cycles taught me that consistent tiny profits add up to huge returns over time.

The psychological hurdles of pattern trading frequently outweigh technological limitations. Maintaining emotional control during drawdowns while waiting for quality setups affects long-term success. Regular review of trading journals aids in identifying and correcting behavioural problems that impede performance.

Pattern recognition improves with screen time and experience. Each market session provides opportunities to study pattern formation and completion. Successful traders mix technical analysis with market psychology knowledge gained over years of observation.

Risk management adaptation is critical for changing market conditions. Position sizing accounts for volatility, whereas stop placement reflects current market behaviour.

These dynamic modifications ensure consistent risk exposure across trading settings.

The journey to trading mastery never completely ends. Markets bring novel difficulties that necessitate ongoing learning and adaptation. Your success is dependent on remaining adaptable while building on established trading ideas.

Multiple elements must be balanced at the same time when executing a trade. Technical analysis, risk management, and psychological control work together to achieve profitable results. Each trade offers opportunities to improve the intricate interaction of trading elements.

Chapter 12

Beyond the basics

Developing Your Own Pattern Recognition Skills

Pattern recognition evolves differently for each trader. After years of market monitoring, I gained an intuitive sense for pattern creation and fulfilment. Trading EUR/USD taught me that patterns typically differ somewhat from textbook examples; these nuances can only be revealed by lengthy chart research and real-world trading experience.

Deliberate practice helps you improve your pattern recognition abilities.

Begin with fundamental patterns on daily charts, where the price activity appears smoother. My early emphasis on simple patterns such as double tops and bottoms laid the groundwork for recognising more complicated formations later.

Developing a Pattern-Based Trading Plan

A comprehensive trading plan converts pattern recognition into consistent profits. The plan should include pattern detection, validation criteria, entry rules, position sizing, and exit options. Trading GBP/USD successfully necessitated precise standards for all aspects of trades execution.

Your trading strategy adjusts to your individual strengths and market conditions. Some traders excel at trend-following patterns, whereas others like reversal settings. After experimenting with several tactics on the USD/JPY,

I noticed that trading continuation patterns in established trends produced the biggest profits.

Advanced Money Management Techniques.

Money management complexity grows with trading experience. Beyond simple position size, advanced strategies involve scaling into positions and managing several connected trades. One winning strategy involves progressively entering USD/CHF bets as pattern confirmation emerges.

Portfolio heat management becomes critical with several investments. Understanding the correlation between currency pairs minimises overexposure to comparable market movements. My trading results considerably improved once I implemented portfolio-level risk controls in addition to individual trades management.

Long-term Success Strategies.

To achieve long-term trading success, process must take precedence over outcomes. Regardless of the most recent results, each trade adheres to established regulations. Despite the difficulties of trading AUD/USD, keeping systematic execution resulted in consistent profitability.

Through pattern specialisation, your trading edge grows. Instead of trading every pattern, concentrate on learning select settings that are compatible with your abilities and personality. My own advantage came from trading harmonic patterns in trending markets under tight validation requirements.

Continuous Education and Improvement

Market evolution necessitates ongoing learning and adaptation.

Patterns that worked well in the past may become ineffective if market conditions shift. Regular review of trading results reveals which patterns remain profitable across market cycles.

Pattern trading success necessitates both technical and psychological growth. Understanding market structure combined with emotional control yields consistent results. Years of trading NZD/USD revealed that psychological improvement is often more important than technical perfection.

The journey to expert pattern trading is never fully over. Every market session provides new insights and learning opportunities. My most useful lessons were generally learnt by analysing pattern failures rather than successful trades.

Advanced pattern traders understand that market environment impacts pattern reliability. The same pattern produces varied results depending on the environment. Trading cross-pairs taught me to evaluate patterns in the context of a larger market, rather than in isolation.

Excelling at pattern trading requires a wide range of abilities and disciplines. Technical analysis, risk management, and psychological control work together to produce profitable results. Success comes from developing these qualities simultaneously while focussing on consistent execution.

Your trading style will organically evolve as you gain experience. Mechanical rule-following develops into intuitive pattern recognition. This evolution takes place gradually over countless hours of chart research and actual trading.

Patience and perseverance are required to achieve pattern trading mastery. Quick profits frequently lead to quick losses, whereas consistent improvement promotes long-term success. My own journey from struggling novice to consistent prosperity required years of concentrated effort and learning from failures.

Advanced traders maintain flexibility while adhering to established norms. Markets evolve, but fundamental patterns in human behaviour stay. Understanding the balance between adaptation and consistency leads to long-term trading success.

The final stage of pattern trading skill goes beyond mechanical rules. Pattern recognition becomes second nature, and risk management remains systematic. This mix of intuitive understanding and rigorous execution provides the best trading results.

Conclusion

Understanding the Art and Science of Pattern Trading

Core Pattern Trading Principles

The book's thorough examination of pattern trading uncovers important insights regarding market mastery. While technical patterns are important, they are merely the first step towards more advanced trading. Each price formation reveals a deeper tale about market psychology, highlighting the constant fight between buyers and sellers. Through years of trading EUR/USD, I've seen how these patterns reflect not only price levels, but also the collective behaviour of market players.

The Development of Pattern Trading Skills

As a pattern trader, you will evolve naturally from basic formations to complicated setups. My adventure started with simple USD/JPY candlestick patterns before progressing to advanced harmonic patterns and multi-timeframe analysis. This continuous progression increases competence and confidence while ensuring effective risk control.

Risk Management Foundation

The foundation of sustainable trading is effective risk management. Perfect pattern recognition is meaningless without accurate position sizing and emotional control. Through harsh lessons in trading GBP/USD, I learnt that capital preservation takes precedence above profit maximisation. This essential idea guides all aspects of professional trading activities.

Integration of Technical Tools.

Advanced pattern trading necessitates the integration of several analytical tools. Technical indicators, volume analysis, and market environment work together to generate strong confirmation signals. Trading cross-pairs highlighted how confluence of several elements determines the most likely setups. This comprehensive approach eliminates out weak patterns while emphasising big opportunities.

Patience & Selectivity

Pattern trading proficiency necessitates extreme patience and accurate selection.

Waiting for optimum settings is often more important than technical expertise in determining profitability. Thousands of hours spent analysing AUD/USD charts have taught me that fewer, higher-quality trades consistently beat frequent trading of marginal patterns.

Psychological Development

The psychological component of pattern trading frequently distinguishes success from failure. Profitable traders are those who manage their emotions, maintain discipline, and adhere to systematic procedures. Trading through tumultuous markets revealed that emotional control is more important than technical proficiency.

Market Adaptation

Long-term success requires ongoing market adaption. Patterns that have previously worked may no longer be successful if market conditions change. Trading numerous currency pairings revealed that distinct patterns perform better in trending versus range markets. This flexibility, when combined with sound principles, yields long-term results.

Trading System Integration

Pattern trading expertise derives from the integration of different disciplines. Technical analysis provides the framework, risk management protects capital, and psychological control ensures consistency in execution. These parts work together to provide a complete approach to market opportunities.

Continuous Learning

The route to pattern trading proficiency changes your entire market approach. Mechanical pattern detection gives way to an intuitive grasp of market dynamics. My most profound discoveries came from analysing unsuccessful patterns and comprehending the market factors that drove them to fail.

Professional Approach

To be successful in pattern trading, you must approach it like a business. Professional traders keep thorough records, manage risks properly, and constantly improve their skills. These professional habits must be developed in order to make the transition from struggling rookie to consistently profitable.

Future Development

Your pattern trading quest will never fully finish. Every market session provides new insights and learning opportunities. The most significant lessons are typically learnt from pattern failures rather than wins. This ongoing development approach influences long-term trading success.

Final Thoughts

The combination of technical capabilities, risk management, and psychological control produces long-term trading performance. swift profits frequently lead to swift losses, whereas consistent improvement fosters long-term success. This journey changes not only your trading, but also your whole understanding of market behaviour and risk management.

Remember that pattern trading mastery is a combination of art and science. Technical correctness is vital, but intuitive market awareness is just as important. Continue to improve your talents, be committed to continual learning, and keep strict discipline in your approach. The markets will test your resolve, but persistence and systematic improvement result in persistent profitability.

Video Access Page

Thank you for purchasing my book! As a token of my appreciation, I've made available exclusive video content just for you.

To access your complimentary videos, simply visit:

https://mega.nz/folder/IYZRQZTL#UIoA3WK6Gb_OfS2Xxq-iRA

Thank you for your support, and I hope these additional resources enhance your reading experience!

Best regards,

James willy